Reading Comprehension Grade 8

Tips and Practice for Reading Assessment

AUTHORS: SCHYRLET CAMERON and SUZANNE MYERS
EDITOR: MARY DIETERICH
PROOFREADERS: MARGARET BROWN and ALEXIS FEY

COPYRIGHT © 2022 Mark Twain Media, Inc.

ISBN 978-1-62223-867-5

Printing No. CD-405075

Mark Twain Media, Inc., Publishers
Distributed by Carson Dellosa Education

Table of Contents

Introduction 1

Test-Taking Tips
    Keys to Success 2
    Ten Strategies for Success 3
    Ten Strategies for Poetry Comprehension/Poetry Terms to Know.....................4
    Technology Skills Self-Assessment 5

Instructional Resources
    Reading Comprehension 6
    Making Inferences 7
    Textual Evidence..8
    Theme 9
    Central Idea 10
    Summary 11
    Word Meaning 12
    Tone 13
    Author's Purpose 14
    Point of View 15
    Organizational Text Structures...16
    Structure of Poetry 17

Practice Assessments
    <u>Literature</u>
        Novel: *The Call of the Wild* by Jack London (adapted)....................................18
        Poem: "I Wandered Lonely as a Cloud" (aka "Daffodils")
            by William Wordsworth...24
        Drama: *Through the Looking Glass* by Lewis Carroll (adapted) 27
    <u>Informational Text</u>
        Speech: "Give Me Liberty or Give Me Death" by Patrick Henry.......................34
        Autobiography: *Up From Slavery* by Booker T. Washington 39
        Science Article: "Pacific Salmon"
            (U.S. Fish & Wildlife Service National Digital Library)..........................43
        Newspaper Article: "The Rights of Women"
            by Frederick Douglass 47
        Flyer (Functional Text): "10th Annual Statewide Middle School
            Science Fair"..51
    <u>Paired Text</u>
        "Grand Commander of the Union Armies" by William H. Mace
            (Secondary Source) 54
        Personal Memoirs of U.S. Grant by Ulysses S. Grant
            (Primary Source) 56

Answer Keys **60**

Introduction

Reading Comprehension, Grade 8 focuses on building fluency and proficiency in essential reading concepts. It is designed to help eighth-grade students strengthen and practice their reading comprehension skills and develop strategies needed to successfully perform on standardized assessments (online or print).

The book is divided into three sections.

◊   The **Test-Taking Tips** section includes tips on preparing for and taking assessments.

◊   The **Instructional Resources** section contains 12 mini-lessons. Each lesson focuses on a different reading comprehension skill, such as making inferences, recognizing point of view, or citing evidence. Each lesson has a short reading passage followed by a sample assessment question. Included in the lesson is a test-taking tip or strategy to help students determine the best way to answer a question.

◊   The **Practice Assessments** section provides students with opportunities to practice their test-taking skills. Each test has a reading selection followed by selected- and constructed-response questions similar to the types of assessment items found on standardized tests. The literature and informational text reading selections cover three types of text: descriptive, expository, and narrative. Some of the text selections are primary sources. This section is divided into three parts.

•   <u>**Literature:**</u> includes novel, poem, and drama reading selections

•   <u>**Informational Text:**</u> includes speech, autobiography, science article, newspaper article, and flyer (functional text) reading selections

•   <u>**Paired Text:**</u> includes two reading selections (primary source and secondary source) on a related topic

Test-Taking Tips

Keys to Success

➤ Be confident and maintain a positive attitude.

➤ Manage your time wisely.

➤ Read or listen to all directions.

➤ Read each question carefully.

➤ Read all answer choices before choosing one.

➤ Eliminate wrong choices, then choose the best answer.

➤ Use details or evidence to support a written response.

➤ Skip or flag difficult questions and answer them last.

➤ Review your answers.

➤ Make sure you have answered all questions.

➤ Think twice before changing an answer.

Test-Taking Tips

Ten Strategies for Success

1. Preview the reading selection for organizational structures and text features.

2. Read all titles, headings, subheadings, maps, charts, graphs, and diagrams carefully.

3. To help you understand the meaning of the text, create mental pictures of what you are reading.

4. As you read, take notes to help you remember and understand key ideas and details.

5. To help you comprehend difficult text, remember to slow down, re-read, or break the text into small chunks.

6. When determining the theme or central idea of a text, the first sentence, the last sentence, or the title usually provides a clue.

7. When you are trying to figure out a vocabulary word from context, replace the word with each of the answer choices and see which answer makes the most sense.

8. Pay close attention to words or phrases in a question that are underlined or are in bold print.

9. Decide what you think the answer to a question is before reading the choices. Then look in order to see if your answer is there.

10. When a question contains the word *best,* remember that there is probably more than one possible answer. You need to look for the **BEST** answer.

Adapted from *Preparing Students for Standardized Testing, Grade 6* by Janet P. Sitter. Used with permission of Mark Twain Media, Inc. Publishers.

Test-Taking Tips

Ten Strategies for Poetry Comprehension

1. **Preview:** Read the title, predict what the poem is about, and identify the poet.
2. **Read:** Read the poem multiple times, both silently and aloud.
3. **Create Mental Pictures:** Visualize what is being described in the poem.
4. **Examine Word Choice:** Determine the meaning of unfamiliar words.
5. **Paraphrase:** Restate the poem in order to clarify the content.
6. **Analyze Structure and Organization:** Determine the overall organization of lines and stanzas. Notice special usage of punctuation and sentence breaks.
7. **Identify Figurative Language:** Examine the poem for the poet's usage of similes, metaphors, imagery, personification, hyperbole, allusion.
8. **Make Connections:** Link what you already know or have experienced to help understand allusions and symbolism.
9. **Identify Sound Devices:** Note use of rhyme, rhythm, repetition, alliteration, onomatopoeia.
10. **Synthesize:** Determine the theme or central idea of the poem.

Poetry Terms to Know

Alliteration – the repeated use of the same consonant sound at the beginning of words

Allusion – a brief reference to a biblical, historical, literary, or mythological person, place, thing, or idea

Hyperbole – a deliberate use of exaggeration for effect or to emphasize a point

Imagery – the use of words to create a vivid mental picture or physical sensation

Metaphor – a figure of speech that compares two unlike objects or ideas without using the words *like* or *as*

Mood – the emotions and feelings the poem arouses in the reader or audience

Onomatopoeia – a word that sounds like its meaning or mimics a sound

Personification – the giving of human characteristics to an animal, non-living object, or idea

Repetition – the repeated use of a word, phrase, line, or stanza in a poem

Rhyme – the pattern of corresponding sounds at the end of each line of a stanza or poem or the corresponding sounds in words within a line

Rhythm – the sound pattern of a poem

Simile – to compare two different things using the words *like* or *as*

Stanza – a series of lines grouped together and separated from other stanzas by a blank line

Structure – the overall organization of the lines of a poem

Symbolism – the use of words, objects, or actions to represent something

Theme – the main message or central idea of a poem

Tone – the poet's feelings (attitude) toward the subject of the poem

Name: _____ Date: _____

Test-Taking Tips
Technology Skills Self-Assessment

Directions: Read the "Checklist of Skills for Online Assessments" chart. Place a checkmark beside the skills that you can successfully perform. Practice the remaining skills until you become proficient.

Checklist of Skills for Online Assessments

I know how to . . .	
	log in to a computer.
	access the test.
	use function buttons.
	navigate through the text.
	play audio/video clips.
	use the vertical scroll bar.
	drag and drop text.
	highlight text.
	select and deselect answers.
	flag questions for later review.
	create and edit responses.
	submit the test.
	exit the test.

Name: _____ Date: _____

Reading Comprehension

Reading comprehension is the ability to understand what you are reading.

 TIP When the text becomes difficult or confusing, remember to slow down, re-read, or break the text into small chunks. Creating a mental picture of what you are reading also helps with comprehension.

Directions: Read the text and answer the sample assessment question.

Text: *Roughing It* by Mark Twain

"HERE HE COMES!"

Every neck is stretched further, and every eye strained wider. Away across the endless dead level of the prairie a black speck appears against the sky, and it is plain that it moves. Well, I should think so!

In a second or two it becomes a horse and rider, rising and falling, rising and falling—sweeping toward us nearer and nearer—growing more and more distinct, more and more sharply defined—nearer and still nearer, and the flutter of the hoofs comes faintly to the ear—another instant a whoop and a hurrah from our upper deck, a wave of the rider's hand, but no reply, and man and horse burst past our excited faces, and go winging away like a belated fragment of a storm!

 So sudden is it all, and so like a flash of unreal fancy, that but for the flake of white foam left quivering and perishing on a mail-sack after the vision had flashed by and disappeared, we might have doubted whether we had seen any actual horse and man at all, maybe.

Public Domain

Sample Assessment Question

Which statement **best** describes the reaction of the spectators to the passing of the horse and rider?

○ A. The spectators ignored the passing of the horse and rider.
○ B. The spectators were grateful that the horse and rider had successfully delivered the mail.
○ C. The spectators were disappointed that the horse and rider did not stop to talk.
● D. The spectators reacted enthusiastically as the horse and rider passed by.

Name: _____ Date: _____

Making Inferences

An **inference** is a conclusion based on reasoning and textual evidence. The reader makes an inference when trying to figure out something the author has not stated explicitly in the text.

 TIP ➤ To make an inference, use clues from the text and what you already know about the topic.

Directions: Read the text and answer the sample assessment questions.

> **Text:** "President" by Mark A. Strange (adapted)
>
> The Constitution set forth certain requirements to be the President of the United States. A person must be a natural-born citizen of the United States. The person may not be an immigrant. He or she must be at least 35 years old and a resident of the United States for at least 14 years.
>
> The 25th Amendment outlines what is done when the president dies, resigns, or is removed from office. The vice president assumes the power of the presidency first; if he or she is unable, then the speaker of the House of Representatives takes over. After the speaker, the next person in line is the president pro tempore of the Senate. Next the various Cabinet department heads are in line for succession, beginning with the secretary of state.
>
> *Understanding the U.S. Constitution* by Mark A. Strange. Used with permission of Mark Twain Media, Inc., Publishers

Sample Assessment Questions

Part A
Based upon the text, what can the reader **infer** about the presidential line of succession?
- ○ A. The speaker of the House comes before the president pro tempore of the Senate in the presidential line for succession. — *Not inference* —
- ◉ B. A foreign-born secretary of state is skipped in the line of succession.
- ○ C. The vice president follows the president in the line of succession.
- ○ D. The 25th amendment is the most important amendment in the Constitution because it establishes the line of succession. *opinion*

Part B
Which statement from the text **most strongly** supports the answer in Part A?
- ◉ A. "A person must be a natural-born citizen of the United States."
- ○ B. "He or she must be at least 35 years old… ."
- ○ C. "The vice president assumes the power of the presidency first; … ."
- ○ D. "The 25th Amendment outlines what is done when the President dies, resigns, or is removed from office."

Name: _____ Date: _____

Textual Evidence

Textual evidence is the information within the text that supports the author's claim or argument.

 TIP To identify evidence or supporting details, search the text for facts, reasons, and statements that support the claim of the author.

Directions: Read the text and answer the sample assessment question.

Text: "The Red Cross Society in Times of Peace" by William H. Mace

[*The following excerpt was published in 1916.*]

It was Clara Barton's firm belief that the world needed the services of the Red Cross in times of peace as well as in times of war. Accordingly an amendment was made to the Geneva treaty. Local Red Cross societies sprang up in every part of the country. The suffering which followed the great Charleston earthquake, the Galveston flood, forest fires, mine explosions, and every similar calamity found the Red Cross Society on hand with aid and supplies.

The greatest calamity that has befallen our country since the Red Cross was well organized was the burning of San Francisco following the great earthquake of 1906. Five hundred millions in property was destroyed, and two hundred and fifty thousand people were left homeless and without food.

Public Domain (*A Beginner's History* by William H. Mace, 1916)

Sample Assessment Question

In the excerpt, the author claims "the burning of San Francisco following the great earthquake of 1906" was the "greatest calamity that has befallen our country since the Red Cross was well organized."

What **two** details from the text show the claim is based on sound reasoning?

Write your answer in the box.

"Five hundred millions in property was destroyed..."
"two hundred and fifty thousand people were left homeless and without food."

Name: _____ Date: _____

Theme

The **theme** is the main message or moral of a story or poem. Some common themes are freedom, survival, friendship, and patriotism.

 TIP To help determine the theme of a text, you must identify its main idea.

Directions: Read the text and answer the sample assessment questions.

Text: *The Red Badge of Courage* by Stephen Crane

    The youth was in a little trance of astonishment. So they were at last going to fight. On the morrow, perhaps, there would be a battle, and he would be in it. For a time he was obliged to labor to make himself believe. He could not accept with assurance an omen that he was about to mingle in one of those great affairs of the earth.

    He had, of course, dreamed of battles all his life—of vague and bloody conflicts that had thrilled him with their sweep and fire. In visions he had seen himself in many struggles. He had imagined peoples secure in the shadow of his eagle-eyed prowess. But awake he had regarded battles as crimson blotches on the pages of the past. He had put them as things of the bygone with his thought-images of heavy crowns and high castles. There was a portion of the world's history which he had regarded as the time of wars, but it, he thought, had been long gone over the horizon and had disappeared forever.

    From his home his youthful eyes had looked upon the war in his own country with distrust. It must be some sort of a play affair. He had long despaired of witnessing a Greeklike struggle. Such would be no more, he had said. Men were better, or more timid. Secular and religious education had effaced the throat-grappling instinct, or else firm finance held in check the passions.

Public Domain

Sample Assessment Questions

Part A
Which word **best** reflects the theme of the text?

- ○ A. defeat
- ○ B. peace
- ⊘ C. war
- ○ D. victory

Part B
Highlight **two** details from the text that **most strongly** support the answer in Part A.

Name: _____ Date: _____

Central Idea

The **central idea** is the most important idea of a text. Nonfiction works may contain multiple central ideas.

 The central or main idea is often revealed by the title or in the first or last sentences of the text. Other times, it is revealed through the key details in the text.

Directions: Read the text and answer the sample assessment question.

Text: "Calcium and Bones" by Schyrlet Cameron and Carolyn Craig (adapted)

Building and maintaining strong bones depends on the mineral calcium. Our body needs calcium to build strong, healthy teeth and bones. During childhood and adolescence, bones grow the most. It is important to get enough calcium during these years. The more bone mass accumulated early in life, the less likely one would be of developing a serious bone problem.

Low calcium levels can cause the likelihood of broken bones, unhealthy teeth, and even rickets. As an adult, low levels of calcium can cause osteoporosis, a painful condition caused by the decrease in bone density (the amount of minerals, especially calcium, in bones). The elderly may experience broken hips and other fractures with decreased bone density.

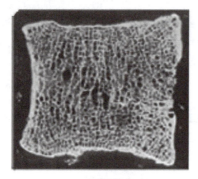   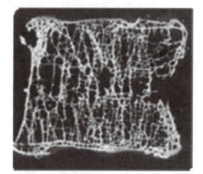

Normal bone   ***Bone with osteoporosis***

Scientific Method Investigation by Schyrlet Cameron and Carolyn Craig. Used with permission of Mark Twain Media, Inc., Publishers.

Sample Assessment Question

How does the author develop the central idea of the text?
- ○ A. The author reveals the most important time for bone development.
- ○ B. The author describes the symptoms of osteoporosis.
- ◉ C. The author explains the connection between calcium and bone development.
- ○ D. The author recommends foods that are good sources of calcium.

Name: _____ Date: _____

Summary

A **summary** contains the key points of a text. It should not include the writer's personal feelings, opinions, or prior knowledge of the subject.

 A summary is usually three or four sentences that include the central idea of a text with supporting details.

Directions: Read the text and answer the sample assessment question.

Text: "Bacteria: The Good, the Bad, and the Ugly" by Anne Davies and Kerry Humes (adapted)

Bacteria are found everywhere. Some bacteria help us digest food. Others are needed to make cheese, sour cream, and yogurt, among other foods. These bacteria are good for us. Other bacteria can cause food poisoning. The symptoms of food poisoning include diarrhea, fever, chills, nausea, vomiting, and abdominal cramps.

Salmonella is harmful bacteria found in raw eggs, undercooked chicken or turkey, and improperly processed lunch meats. If you ingest the *Salmonella* bacteria, symptoms usually start 8 to 12 hours later. Most people will be sick for three to five days and usually do not require medical treatment. Avoid this bad bacteria by cooking your food thoroughly.

Healthy Eating & Exercise by Anne Davies and Kerry Humes. Used with permission of Mark Twain Media, Inc., Publishers.

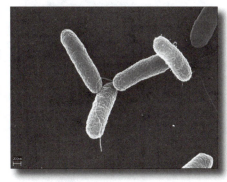

Salmonella typhimurium bacteria

Sample Assessment Question

Which **two** statements should be included in a summary of the text?
- ⊘ A. Bacteria are either beneficial or harmful to humans.
- ⊘ B. Proper handling of food helps prevent the growth of bacteria.
- ○ C. Avoid food poisoning by cooking your food properly.
- ○ D. Nausea and vomiting are symptoms of food poisoning.
- ○ E. Symptoms of food poisoning appear 8 to 12 hours after ingesting the *Salmonella* bacteria.
- ○ F. Bad bacteria, like *Salmonella*, can cause food poisoning.

Name: _____ Date: _____

Word Meaning

As you read, you may encounter unfamiliar words.

 TIP ➤ Use context clues to help you determine the meaning of an unfamiliar word. The context is the other words, phrases, and sentences that surround the unfamiliar word.

Directions: Read the text and answer the sample assessment questions.

Text: *Gulliver's Travels* by Jonathan Swift

 I lay down on the grass, which was very short and soft, where I slept sounder than ever I remembered to have done in my life, and, as I reckoned, about nine hours; for when I awaked, it was just day-light. I attempted to rise, but was not able to stir: for, as I happened to lie on my back, I found my arms and legs were strongly fastened on each side to the ground; and my hair, which was long and thick, tied down in the same manner. I likewise felt several slender ligatures across my body, from my arm-pits to my thighs. I could only look upwards; the sun began to grow hot, and the light offended my eyes. I heard a confused noise about me; but in the posture I lay, could see nothing except the sky. In a little time I felt something alive moving on my left leg, which advancing gently forward over my breast, came almost up to my chin; when, bending my eyes downwards as much as I could, I perceived it to be a human creature not six inches high, with a bow and arrow in his hands, and a quiver at his back.

Public Domain

Sample Assessment Questions

Part A
What is the **best** meaning of the word <u>ligatures</u> as it is used in the text?
- ○ A. holder for arrows
- ○ B. muscle of the human body
- ○ C. object used to tie or fasten
- ⊘ D. thin ropes

Part B
Which **two** phrases from the text **best** help the reader determine the meaning of <u>ligatures</u>?
- ○ A. "attempted to rise"
- ○ B. "not able to stir"
- ⊘ C. "strongly fastened"
- ⊘ D. "tied down"
- ○ E. "arm-pits to my thighs"
- ○ F. "quiver at his back"

Name: _____ Date: _____

Tone

Tone is how an author feels toward the topic or subject of the text. Authors create tone by using words with positive or negative connotations. They also use figurative language, such as similes, metaphors, and personification. Examples of words that describe tone are *cheery, angry, amused,* and *sad.*

 Look closely at the author's choice of words. Identify the connotation of words and search for examples of figurative language.

Directions: Read the text and answer the sample assessment questions.

Text: *White Fang* by Jack London

Dark spruce forest frowned on either side the frozen waterway. The trees had been stripped by a recent wind of their white covering of frost, and they seemed to lean towards each other, black and ominous, in the fading light. A vast silence reigned over the land. The land itself was desolation, lifeless, without movement, so lone and cold that the spirit of it was not even that of sadness. It was the Wild, the savage, frozen-hearted Northland Wild.

Public Domain

Sample Assessment Questions

Part A
Which word **best** describes the tone of the text?
- ○ A. sad
- ⊗ B. gloomy
- ⊘ C. scary
- ⊗ D. serious

Part B
Select the **two** details from the text that **best** support the answer in Part A.
- ○ A. "stripped by a recent wind"
- ○ B. "white covering of frost"
- ○ C. "seemed to lean towards each other"
- ◉ D. "black and ominous, in the fading light"
- ◉ E. "desolation, lifeless, without movement"
- ○ F. "it was not even that of sadness"

Name: _____ Date: _____

Author's Purpose

The **author's purpose** is the reason an author writes about a specific topic.

TIP ▶ To determine the author's purpose, ask yourself these questions:

- Did the author try to amuse me? (Entertain)
- Did the author try to teach me about something? (Inform/Explain)
- Did the author try to influence me by giving an opinion? (Persuade)
- Did the author give details to make something clear? (Describe)

Directions: Read the text and answer the sample assessment question.

Text: "Ratification and a New Republic" by George Lee (adapted)

In order to become a law, the new Constitution would have to be ratified by the states. People began taking sides for or against the ratification of the new Constitution. Those who approved of the new Constitution were called Federalists. This group believed in a strong central government with the power to tax and regulate interstate commerce. The Anti-Federalists felt the new Constitution should be rejected. They believed the states were giving up too much power. They felt the taxing power was too broad. Without a bill of rights, they also feared that the new government would become a tyranny like England had been.

The American Revolution by George Lee. Used with permission of Mark Twain Media, Inc., Publishers.

Sample Assessment Question

What is the author's purpose for writing the text?
- ○ A. to analyze the Anti-Federalist position on ratification of the Constitution.
- ○ B. to describe the steps required for ratification of the Constitution.
- ◉ C. to explain the positions of the Federalists and Anti-Federalists on ratification of the Constitution.
- ○ D. to persuade the reader to agree with the Federalists' position on ratification of the Constitution.

Name: _____ Date: _____

Point of View

Point of view is the perspective from which something is written or told. Depending on the type of writing, the point of view expresses the thoughts, feelings, and beliefs of a narrator, character, author, or speaker.

 TIP ➤ To help identify the point of view, look at the personal pronouns used in the text. Words like *I* and *we* are used with **first-person** point of view. Words like *he, she,* and *it* help to identify **third-person** point of view.

Directions: Read the text and answer the sample assessment question.

Text: *The Voyages of Doctor Dolittle* by Hugh Lofting

I wondered if it were supper-time yet. Of course I had no watch of my own, but I noticed a gentleman coming towards me down the road; and when he got nearer I saw it was the Colonel out for a walk. He was all wrapped up in smart overcoats and mufflers and bright-colored gloves. It was not a very cold day but he had so many clothes on he looked like a pillow inside a roll of blankets. I asked him if he would please tell me the time.

He stopped, grunted and glared down at me— his red face growing redder still; and when he spoke it sounded like the cork coming out of a gingerbeer-bottle.

"Do you imagine for one moment," he spluttered, "that I am going to get myself all unbuttoned just to tell a little boy like you THE TIME!" And he went stumping down the street, grunting harder than ever.

Public Domain

Sample Assessment Question

How does the point of view used by the author most likely effect how the reader feels about the Colonel's response to the boy's request?
- ○ A. The reader feels sympathy for the boy.
- ○ B. The reader understands the Colonel's anger.
- ◉ C. The reader sees the serious nature of the situation.
- ○ D. The reader believes the boy's request is unreasonable.

Name: _____ Date: _____

Organizational Text Structures

Text structures are organizational patterns used to break information down into parts that can be easily understood by the reader.

Common Organizational Text Structures

Definition	Classification	Description
Compare/Contrast examines how concepts and events are alike and different. Signal words/phrases: *alike, different, same, compare to*	**Classification** divides topics into related categories or groups. Signal words/phrases: *group, divide, sort, classify, type*	**Description** describes something using details and/or examples. Signal words/phrases: *such as, for example, looks like*
Argument/Support states a point of view and supports it with details or evidence. Signal words/phrases: *I believe, in my opinion, I think*	**Cause/Effect** presents a major idea or event and resulting effects. Signal words/phrases: *because of, as a result of, due to, causing*	**Chronological/Sequential** arranges events in time order or a list of steps in a process. Signal words/phrases: *in, by, later, then, before, finally, first, next, now, after, last*

| | **Definition** introduces and explains a word or concept. Signal words/phrases: *is, for example, also, can be, in fact* | **Problem/Solution** states a problem and gives possible solutions. Signal words/phrases: *question is, answer is, problem is* |

TIP Use signal words and phrases to help identify organizational text structures.

Directions: Read the text and answer the sample assessment question.

Text: "Life of the Lower Classes in the Renaissance" by Patrick Hotle

The close quarters and unhealthy atmosphere of cities during the Renaissance account for the effects of the Bubonic Plague, better known as the Black Death. This disease was carried by fleas on rats. Cities in the late Middle Ages and Renaissance had huge populations of these rodents living off garbage and nesting in rafters. Infected fleas easily dropped onto the humans below. This killed approximately one-third of Europe's population between 1348 and 1350.

Renaissance by Patrick Hotle. Used with permission of Mark Twain Media, Inc., Publishers.

Sample Assessment Question

Which type of structure **best** describes the way the text is organized?
- ○ A. cause/effect
- ○ B. compare/contrast
- ○ C. chronological/sequential
- ○ D. description

Name: _____ Date: _____

Structure of Poetry

The **structure of a poem** is the overall organization of the lines. Lines of a poem may vary in length. A poet may choose to place an entire sentence on one line or break the sentence into multiple lines.

Stanzas are a series of lines grouped together and are separated from other stanzas by a blank line. Each stanza conveys an idea similar to paragraphs in an essay. A stanza may vary in the number of lines. Common types of stanzas are **couplets** (two rhyming lines), **tercets** (three lines that may or may not rhyme), and **quatrains** (four lines that may or may not rhyme). Many modern poems are **free verse**; they may not have any identifiable structure.

 Determine the overall organization of lines and stanzas. Notice special usage of punctuation and sentence breaks.

Directions: Read the poem and follow the directions below.

Poem: "A Poison Tree" by William Blake

> I was angry with my friend:
> I told my wrath, my wrath did end.
> I was angry with my foe:
> I told it not, my wrath did grow.
>
> And I watered it in fears
> Night and morning with my tears,
> And I sunned it with smiles
> And with soft deceitful wiles.
>
> And it grew both day and night,
> Till it bore an apple bright,
> And my foe beheld it shine,
> And he knew that it was mine,--
>
> And into my garden stole
> When the night had veiled the pole;
> In the morning, glad, I see
> My foe outstretched beneath the tree.

Public Domain

Sample Assessment Questions

1. Write the number of stanzas in the poem. _____
2. Write the number of lines in each stanza. _____
3. Circle a sentence in the poem that is broken into multiple lines.
4. Which word in the poem rhymes with **night**? _____

Name: _____ Date: _____

Novel

Directions: Read the text and answer the questions.

Text: *The Call of the Wild* by Jack London (adapted)

(John Thornton, owner of the dog, Buck, had said that Buck could draw a sled loaded with one thousand pounds of flour. Another miner bet sixteen hundred dollars that he couldn't, and Thornton, though fearing it would be too much for Buck, was ashamed to refuse; so he let Buck try to draw a load that Matthewson's team of ten dogs had been hauling.)

The team of ten dogs was unhitched, and Buck, with his own harness, was put into the sled. He had felt the general excitement, and he felt that in some way he must do a great thing for John Thornton. Murmurs of admiration at his splendid appearance went up. He was in perfect condition, without an ounce of superfluous flesh, and the one hundred and fifty pounds that he weighed were so many pounds of grit and virility. His furry coat shone with the sheen of silk. Down the neck and across the shoulders, his mane, in repose as it was, half bristled and seemed to lift with every movement, as though excess of vigor made each particular hair alive and active. The great breast and heavy forelegs were no more than in proportion with the rest of the body, where the muscles showed in tight rolls underneath the skin. Men felt these muscles and proclaimed them hard as iron, and the odds went down two to one.

"Sir, sir," stuttered a member of the latest dynasty, a king of the Skookum Benches. "I offer you eight hundred for him, sir, before the test, sir; eight hundred just as he stands."

Thornton shook his head and stepped to Buck's side.

"You must stand off from him," Matthewson protested. "Free play and plenty of room."

The crowd fell silent; only could be heard the voices of the gamblers vainly offering two to one. Everybody acknowledged Buck a magnificent animal, but twenty fifty-pound sacks of flour bulked too large in their eyes for them to loosen their pouch-strings.

Thornton knelt down by Buck's side. He took his head into his two hands and rested cheek on cheek. He did not playfully shake him, as he was wont, or murmur soft love curses; but he whispered in his ear. "As you love me, Buck. As you love me," was what he whispered. Buck whined with suppressed eagerness.

The crowd was watching curiously. The affair was growing mysterious. It seemed like a conjuration. As Thornton got to his feet, Buck seized his mittened hand between his jaws, pressing in with his teeth and releasing slowly, half-reluctantly. It was the answer, in terms, not of speech, but of love. Thornton stepped well back.

"Now, Buck," he said.

Name: _____ Date: _____

Novel (cont.)

Buck tightened the traces, then slacked them for a matter of several inches. It was the way he had learned.

"Gee!" Thornton's voice rang out, sharp in the tense silence.

Buck swung to the right, ending the movement in a plunge that took up the slack and with a sudden jerk arrested his one hundred and fifty pounds. The load quivered, and from under the runners arose a crisp crackling.

"Haw!" Thornton commanded.

Buck duplicated the maneuver, this time to the left. The crackling turned into a snapping, the sled pivoting and the runners slipping and grating several inches to the side.

The sled was broken out. Men were holding their breaths, intensely unconscious of the fact.

"Now, MUSH!"

Thornton's command cracked out like a pistol-shot. Buck threw himself forward, tightening the traces with a jarring lunge. His whole body was gathered tightly together in a tremendous effort, the muscles writhing and knotting like live things under the silky fur. His great chest was low to the ground, his head forward and down, while his feet were flying like mad, the claws scarring the hard-packed snow in parallel grooves. The sled swayed and trembled, half-started forward. One of his feet slipped, and one man groaned aloud. Then the sled lurched ahead in what appeared a rapid succession of jerks, though it really never came to a dead stop again—half an inch—an inch—two inches. The jerks became less as the sled gained momentum, he caught them up, till it was moving steadily along.

Men gasped and began to breathe again, unaware that for a moment they had ceased to breathe. Thornton was running behind, encouraging Buck with short, cheery words. The distance had been measured off, and as he neared the pile of firewood which marked the end of the hundred yards, a cheer began to grow and grow, which burst into a roar as he passed the firewood and halted at command. Every man was tearing himself loose, even Matthewson, who had lost his wager. Hats and mittens were flying in the air. Men were shaking hands, it did not matter with whom, and bubbling over in a general incoherent babel. But Thornton fell on his knees beside Buck. Head was against head, and he was shaking him back and forth.

"Sir! Sir!" spluttered the Skookum Bench king. "I'll give you a thousand for him, sir, a thousand, sir—twelve hundred, sir."

Thornton rose to his feet. His eyes were wet. The tears were streaming frankly down his cheeks. "Sir," he said to the Skookum Bench king, "no, sir. You can hold your tongue, sir. It's the best I can do for you, sir."

Buck seized Thornton's hand in his teeth. Thornton shook him back and forth. As though moved by a common feeling, the onlookers drew back to a respectful distance; nor did they again interrupt.

---

superfluous – unnecessary

dynasty – race or succession of kings

Public Domain ("Buck's Trial of Strength." *Short Stories and Selections for Use in the Secondary Schools.* Compiled by Emilie Kip Baker)

Name: _____ Date: _____

Novel (cont.)

Assessment Questions

1. What is the **main** purpose for the first paragraph of the text?
   - ○ A. to reveal the men's admiration of Buck's physical condition
   - ○ B. to justify the Skookum Bench king's offer of $800 to purchase Buck
   - ○ C. to reveal to the reader Buck's odds of winning the pulling test
   - ○ D. to describe to the reader Buck's physical condition

2. Read the sentence from the text and the directions that follow.

> Down the neck and across the shoulders, his mane, in repose as it was, half bristled and seemed to lift with every movement, as though <u>excess of vigor</u> made each particular hair alive and active.

   Select the **best** meaning of the phrase <u>excess of vigor</u> as it is used in the sentence.
   - ○ A. additional force
   - ○ B. too much power
   - ○ C. surplus of energy
   - ○ D. overload of emotions

3. Which word **best** reflects the theme of the text?
   - ○ A. love
   - ○ B. obedience
   - ○ C. sacrifice
   - ○ D. survival

4. Read the excerpt from the text and answer the question.

> Thornton knelt down by Buck's side. He took his head into his two hands and rested cheek on cheek. He did not playfully shake him, as he was wont, or murmur soft love curses; but he whispered in his ear. "As you love me, Buck. As you love me," was what he whispered. Buck whined with suppressed eagerness.

   How does the excerpt contribute to the development of the theme?
   - ○ A. It demonstrates Buck's willingness to be obedient to his owner's command.
   - ○ B. It demonstrates the loving relationship between Buck and John Thornton.
   - ○ C. It demonstrates Buck's willingness to sacrifice himself for John Thornton.
   - ○ D. It demonstrates Buck's eagerness to survive the challenge.

Name: _____ Date: _____

Novel (cont.)

5. Read the sentence from the text and answer the question.

> Men felt these muscles and proclaimed them hard as iron, and the odds went down two to one.

A simile is a comparison of one thing to another. What was the author's purpose for using a simile in the sentence?
- ○ A. to provide a mental image of Buck's muscles
- ○ B. to demonstrate Buck's strength
- ○ C. to reveal why the gamblers lowered the odds of Buck winning
- ○ D. to describe how Buck's muscles felt to the men

6. Read the excerpt from the text and answer the question.

> The crowd fell silent; only could be heard the voices of the gamblers vainly offering two to one. Everybody acknowledged Buck a magnificent animal, but twenty fifty-pound sacks of flour bulked too large in their eyes for them to loosen their pouch-strings.

What does the excerpt reveal about the crowd?
- ○ A. The crowd doubted Buck's ability to win.
- ○ B. The crowd disapproved of gambling.
- ○ C. The crowd placed bets with the gamblers.
- ○ D. The crowd felt the pulling test was unfair.

7. Read the excerpt from the text and answer the question.

> Thornton knelt down by Buck's side. He took his head into his two hands and rested cheek on cheek. He did not playfully shake him, as he was wont, or murmur soft love curses; but he whispered in his ear. "As you love me, Buck. As you love me," was what he whispered.

Which point of view is used in this excerpt?
- ○ A. The narrator describes Buck's thoughts and feelings.
- ○ B. The narrator describes Thornton's thoughts and feelings.
- ○ C. John Thornton describes Buck's thoughts and feelings.
- ○ D. John Thornton describes his own thoughts and feelings.

Name: _____ Date: _____

Novel (cont.)

8. **Part A**

What was Buck's motive for winning the pulling test?
- ○ A. He wanted to prove that he was the superior sled dog.
- ○ B. He wanted to please the crowd.
- ○ C. He wanted John Thornton to beat Matthewson.
- ○ D. He wanted to please John Thornton.

Part B

Which detail from the text **best** supports the answer in Part A?
- ○ A. "He was in perfect condition, without an ounce of superfluous flesh, and the one hundred and fifty pounds that he weighed were so many pounds of grit and virility."
- ○ B. "He had felt the general excitement, and he felt that in some way he must do a great thing for John Thornton."
- ○ C. "The crowd fell silent; only could be heard the voices of the gamblers vainly offering two to one."
- ○ D. "Buck whined with suppressed eagerness."

9. Read the excerpt and answer the question.

> The distance had been measured off, and as he neared the pile of firewood which marked the end of the hundred yards, a cheer began to grow and grow, which burst into a roar as he passed the firewood and halted at command. Every man was tearing himself loose, even Matthewson, who had lost his wager.

What does the excerpt reveal about Matthewson?
- ○ A. Matthewson was concerned about the noise level of the crowd.
- ○ B. Matthewson was ecstatic about Buck's triumph.
- ○ C. Matthewson was displeased with the crowd's reaction.
- ○ D. Matthewson was angry about losing his wager.

Name: _____ Date: _____

Novel (cont.)

10. Read Excerpt 1 and Excerpt 2 from the text and the directions that follow.

Excerpt 1
The crowd was watching curiously. The affair was growing mysterious. It seemed like a conjuration. As Thornton got to his feet, Buck seized his mittened hand between his jaws, pressing in with his teeth and releasing slowly, half-reluctantly. It was the answer, in terms, not of speech, but of love.

Excerpt 2
Buck seized Thornton's hand in his teeth. Thornton shook him back and forth. As though moved by a common feeling, the onlookers drew back to a respectful distance; nor did they again interrupt.

Explain how Excerpt 1 helps you to understand Buck's motive for seizing Thornton's hand with his teeth in Excerpt 2. Use evidence from the excerpts to support your answer.

Write your answer in the box.

Name: _____ Date: _____

Poem

Directions: Read the text and answer the questions.

Text: "I Wandered Lonely as a Cloud" (aka "Daffodils") by William Wordsworth

I wandered lonely as a cloud
That floats on high o'er vales and hills,
When all at once I saw a crowd,
A host, of golden daffodils;
Beside the lake, beneath the trees,
Fluttering and dancing in the breeze.

Continuous as the stars that shine
And twinkle on the milky way,
They stretched in never-ending line
Along the margin of a bay:
Ten thousand saw I at a glance,
Tossing their heads in sprightly dance.

The waves beside them danced; but they
Out-did the sparkling waves in glee:
A poet could not but be gay,
In such a jocund company:
I gazed—and gazed—but little thought
What wealth the show to me had brought:

For oft, when on my couch I lie
In vacant or in pensive mood,
They flash upon that inward eye
Which is the bliss of solitude;
And then my heart with pleasure fills,
And dances with the daffodils.

Public Domain

Assessment Questions

1. Which **two** lines from the poem help the reader determine the setting of the daffodils.
   - ○ A. *That floats on high o'er vales and hills,*
   - ○ B. *Beside the lake, beneath the trees,*
   - ○ C. *And twinkle on the milky way,*
   - ○ D. *Along the margin of a bay:*
   - ○ E. *For oft, when on my couch I lie*
   - ○ F. *And dances with the daffodils.*

Name: _____ Date: _____

Poem (cont.)

2. Read the dictionary entry and answer the question.

> **host** \hōst\ *n* 1. multitude or huge number 2. one who extends hospitality to another person 3. an army assembled for battle 4. emcee of a television show

Which is the definition for the word *host* as it is used in stanza 1?
- ○ A. definition 1
- ○ B. definition 2
- ○ C. definition 3
- ○ D. definition 4

3. **Part A**
Which word **best** reflects the **key** theme of the poem?
- ○ A. clouds
- ○ B. loneliness
- ○ C. memories
- ○ D. moods

Part B
Which stanza of the poem is the **most** helpful in understanding the **key** theme?
- ○ A. stanza 1
- ○ B. stanza 2
- ○ C. stanza 3
- ○ D. stanza 4

4. Which sentence **best** summarizes the meaning of the poem?
- ○ A. Daffodils are beautiful flowers that bloom in the spring.
- ○ B. Joy can be found in taking long walks along the beach.
- ○ C. Taking long walks is a healthy activity people enjoy.
- ○ D. Even the most insignificant event can create a lasting memory.

5. Read the lines from the poem and answer the question.

> *I gazed—and gazed—but little thought*
> *What wealth the show to me had brought:*

What is **most likely** the significance of the poet's use of repetition?
- ○ A. It emphasizes the length of time the speaker looked at the daffodils.
- ○ B. It demonstrates the speaker's interest in watching the daffodils.
- ○ C. It creates a visual image of the speaker's thoughts and feelings.
- ○ D. It reveals the speaker's lack of interest in viewing the daffodils.

Name: _____ Date: _____

Poem (cont.)

6. **Part A**

Based upon the poem, what generalization can the reader **most likely** make about the speaker?
- ○ A. The speaker enjoys taking long walks in the countryside.
- ○ B. The speaker's favorite flower is the daffodil.
- ○ C. The speaker lives beside a lake.
- ○ D. The speaker is often preoccupied with his own thoughts.

Part B

Which lines from the poem **best** support the answer in Part A?
- ○ A. *I wandered lonely as a cloud / That floats on high o'er vales and hills,*
- ○ B. *They flash upon that inward eye / Which is the bliss of solitude*
- ○ C. *For oft, when on my couch I lie / In vacant or in pensive mood,*
- ○ D. *And then my heart with pleasure fills, / And dances with the daffodils.*

7. Read the two lines from stanza 3 of the poem and answer the question.

> *I gazed—and gazed—but little thought*
> *What wealth the show to me had brought:*

Explain how the two lines from stanza 3 contribute to the meaning of stanza 4. Use textual evidence from the poem to support your answer.

Write your answer in the box.

Name: _____ Date: _____

Drama

Directions: Read the text and answer the questions.

Text: *Through the Looking Glass* by Lewis Carroll (adapted)

ACT I
SCENE TWO

SETTING: *A small clearing in the middle of the woods with a small brook running through.*

CURTAIN RISE: *ALICE is standing in a clear spot in the woods. The stage lights suddenly begin to dim. ALICE looks up at the sky as though she is looking for a thunderstorm to appear.*

ALICE: What a thick black cloud that is! And how fast it comes! Why, I do believe it's got wings! [*Seeing that it is the monstrous crow, ALICE runs under a tree.*] It can never get at me HERE. It's far too large to squeeze itself in among the trees. But I wish it wouldn't flap its wings so—it makes quite a hurricane in the woods—here's somebody's shawl being blown away!

[*ALICE catches the shawl and looks about for the owner. The WHITE QUEEN comes running wildly onto stage, with both arms stretched out wide, as if she were flying. ALICE very civilly goes to meet her with the shawl.*]

ALICE: I'm very glad I happened to be in the way. [*ALICE helps the WHITE QUEEN put on her shawl.*]

WHITE QUEEN: [*The WHITE QUEEN looks at ALICE in a helpless frightened sort of way, and keeps repeatedly whispering the same phrase to herself.*] Bread-and-butter, bread-and-butter, bread-and-butter.

ALICE: [*Timidly*] Am I addressing the White Queen?

WHITE QUEEN: Well, yes, if you call that a-dressing. It isn't my notion of the thing, at all.

ALICE: [*Smiles*] If your Majesty will only tell me the right way to begin, I'll do it as well as I can.

WHITE QUEEN: [*Groans*] But I don't want it done at all. I've been a-dressing myself for the last two hours.

ALICE: Every single thing's crooked, and you're all over pins; may I put your shawl straight for you?

WHITE QUEEN: I don't know what's the matter with it! It's out of temper, I think. I've pinned it here, and I've pinned it there, but there's no pleasing it!

ALICE: It CAN'T go straight, you know, if you pin it all on one side. Dear me, what a state your hair is in!

Name: _____ Date: _____

Drama (cont.)

WHITE QUEEN: The brush has got entangled in it! And I lost the comb yesterday.

ALICE: [*Takes out the brush and arranges the WHITE QUEEN's hair.*] You look better now! But really you should have a lady's maid!

WHITE QUEEN: I'm sure I'll take you with pleasure! Twopence a week and jam every other day.

ALICE: [*Laughs*] I don't want you to hire ME—and I don't care for jam.

WHITE QUEEN: It's very good jam.

ALICE: Well, I don't want any TODAY, at any rate.

WHITE QUEEN: You couldn't have it if you DID want it. The rule is, jam tomorrow and jam yesterday—but never jam today.

ALICE: It MUST come sometimes to "jam today."

WHITE QUEEN: No, it can't. It's jam every OTHER day; today isn't any OTHER day, you know.

ALICE: I don't understand you. It's dreadfully confusing!

WHITE QUEEN: [*Kindly*] That's the effect of living backwards. It always makes one a little giddy at first—

ALICE: Living backwards! I never heard of such a thing!

WHITE QUEEN: —but there's one great advantage in it, that one's memory works both ways.

ALICE: I'm sure MINE only works one way. I can't remember things before they happen.

WHITE QUEEN: It's a poor sort of memory that only works backwards.

ALICE: What sort of things do YOU remember best?

WHITE QUEEN: Oh, things that happened the week after next. [*The WHITE QUEEN begins wrapping a piece of white cloth around her finger.*] For instance, now, there's the King's messenger. He's in prison being punished; and the trial doesn't even begin till next Wednesday; and of course the crime comes last of all.

ALICE: Suppose he never commits the crime?

WHITE QUEEN: [*Binds the cloth with ribbon.*] That would be all the better, wouldn't it?

ALICE: Of course it would be all the better, but it wouldn't be all the better his being punished.

WHITE QUEEN: You're wrong THERE, at any rate; were YOU ever punished?

ALICE: Only for faults.

WHITE QUEEN: And you were all the better for it, I know!

ALICE: Yes, but then I HAD done the things I was punished for; that makes all the difference.

Name: _____ Date: _____

Drama (cont.)

WHITE QUEEN: But if you HADN'T done them that would have been better still; better and better and better!

ALICE: There's a mistake somewhere—

WHITE QUEEN: [*Screams like the whistle of a steam engine, and shakes her hand*] Oh, Oh, Oh! My finger's bleeding. Oh, oh, oh, oh!

ALICE: What IS the matter? Have you pricked your finger?

WHITE QUEEN: I haven't pricked it YET—but I soon shall— oh, oh, oh!

ALICE: [*Trying not to laugh*] When do you expect to do it?

WHITE QUEEN: When I fasten my shawl again; the brooch will come undone directly. Oh, oh! [*Brooch flies open and she clutches it wildly*]

ALICE: Take care! You're holding it all crooked!

WHITE QUEEN: [*Pricks her finger and smiles*] That accounts for the bleeding, you see. Now you understand the way things happen here.

ALICE: But why don't you scream now?

WHITE QUEEN: Why, I've done all the screaming already. What would be the good of having it all over again?

[*The stage lights slowly grow brighter.*]

ALICE: The crow must have flown away, I think. I'm so glad it's gone. I thought it was the night coming on.

WHITE QUEEN: I wish I could manage to be glad! Only I never can remember the rule. You must be very happy, living in this wood, and being glad whenever you like!

ALICE: [*Speaking in a melancholy voice*] Only it is so VERY lonely here! [*Tears roll down her cheeks.*]

WHITE QUEEN: [*Wringing her hands in despair*] Oh, don't go on like that! Consider what a great girl you are. Consider what a long way you've come today. Consider what o'clock it is. Consider anything, only don't cry!

ALICE: [*Laughs*] Can YOU keep from crying by considering things?

WHITE QUEEN: That's the way it's done. Nobody can do two things at once, you know. Let's consider your age to begin with—how old are you?

ALICE: I'm seven and a half exactly.

Name: _____ Date: _____

Drama (cont.)

WHITE QUEEN: You needn't say "exactly." I can believe it without that. Now I'll give YOU something to believe. I'm just one hundred and one, five months and a day.

ALICE: I can't believe THAT!

WHITE QUEEN: [*Speaking in a pitying tone*] Can't you? Try again: draw a long breath, and shut your eyes.

ALICE: [*Laughs*] There's no use trying. One CAN'T believe impossible things.

WHITE QUEEN: I daresay you haven't had much practice. When I was your age, I always did it for half-an-hour a day. Why, sometimes I've believed as many as six impossible things before breakfast. [*The brooch comes undone while she is speaking.*] There goes the shawl again!

[*A sudden gust of wind blows the WHITE QUEEN's shawl across a little brook. The WHITE QUEEN spreads out her arms again, chases after it, and catches the shawl.*]

WHITE QUEEN: I've got it! Now you shall see me pin it on again, all by myself!

ALICE: [*Speaking very politely*] Then I hope your finger is better now?

[*ALICE crosses the little brook after the WHITE QUEEN. They both exit off the stage.*]

Public Domain

Name: _____ Date: _____

Drama (cont.)

Assessment Questions

1. Read the lines from the play and answer the question.

> **ALICE:** It CAN'T go straight, you know, if you pin it all on one side. Dear me, what a state your hair is in!
>
> **WHITE QUEEN:** The brush has got entangled in it! And I lost the comb yesterday.
>
> **ALICE:** [*Takes out the brush and arranges the WHITE QUEEN'S hair.*] You look better now! But really you should have a lady's maid!

What is the playwright **most likely** trying to reveal about the White Queen?
- ○ A. She is careless with her possessions.
- ○ B. She is wealthy enough to hire servants.
- ○ C. She is dependent on others for assistance.
- ○ D. She is not concerned with how she looks.

2. What is **most likely** the playwright's purpose for writing some words of the dialogue in all capital letters?
- ○ A. He is letting the actors know which lines are the most important.
- ○ B. He is using the words to reveal the tone to the audience.
- ○ C. He uses the words to signal a change in the dialogue.
- ○ D. He wants the actor to emphasize the words when speaking.

3. Why is the CURTAIN RISE section of the script important?
- ○ A. It gives the reader a description of who and what will be on stage when an act or scene begins.
- ○ B. It lets the characters know where they will be standing when the curtain rises.
- ○ C. It helps the reader to recognize the main characters in the play.
- ○ D. It summarizes what is going to happen during the scene.

4. Personification is a figure of speech that a writer uses to give human qualities or emotions to animals, ideas, or objects. Which line from the play contains an example of personification?
- ○ A. "But I don't want it done at all. I've been a-dressing myself for the last two hours."
- ○ B. "I don't know what's the matter with it [shawl]! It's out of temper, I think. I've pinned it here, and I've pinned it there, but there's no pleasing it!"
- ○ C. "When I fasten my shawl again; the brooch will come undone directly. Oh, oh!"
- ○ D. "There's no use trying. One CAN'T believe impossible things."

Name: _____ Date: _____

Drama (cont.)

5. Read the lines of dialogue from the play and answer the question.

> ALICE: [*Timidly*] Am I addressing the White Queen?
>
> WHITE QUEEN: Well, yes, if you call that a-dressing. It isn't my notion of the thing, at all.
>
> ALICE: [*Smiles*] If your Majesty will only tell me the right way to begin, I'll do it as well as I can.
>
> WHITE QUEEN: [*Groans*] But I don't want it done at all. I've been a-dressing myself for the last two hours.
>
> ALICE: Every single thing's crooked, and you're all over pins; may I put your shawl straight for you?

Which word **best** describes the tone of the excerpt from the play?
- ○ A. amusing
- ○ B. encouraging
- ○ C. frustrated
- ○ D. sincere

6. Read the lines from the play and answer the question.

> WHITE QUEEN: You're wrong THERE, at any rate; were YOU ever punished?
>
> ALICE: Only for <u>faults</u>.

Which word is the **best** synonym for the word <u>faults</u> as it is used in the line?
- ○ A. errors
- ○ B. failures
- ○ C. mistakes
- ○ D. wrongdoings

Name: _____ Date: _____

Drama (cont.)

7. Based on the play, explain the concept of "living backwards" using the events that surround the White Queen, her shawl, and the brooch. Support your answer with textual evidence.

   Write your answer in the box.

Name: _____ Date: _____

Speech

Directions: Read the speech and answer the questions.

Text: "Give Me Liberty or Give Me Death" by Patrick Henry

(*On March 23, 1775, a month before the Battle of Lexington, Patrick Henry electrified the Virginia convention with the speech that here follows. A resolution was before the convention "that the colony be immediately put in a state of defense." The speech is Henry's response to the resolution.*)

Mr. President, it is natural to man to indulge in the illusions of hope. We are apt to shut our eyes against a painful truth, and listen to the song of that siren till she transforms us into beasts. Is this the part of wise men engaged in a great and arduous struggle for liberty? Are we disposed to be of the number of those who, having eyes see not, and having ears hear not, the things which so nearly concern their temporal salvation? For my part, whatever anguish of spirit it may cost, I am willing to know the whole truth; to know the worst and to provide for it.

I have but one lamp by which my feet are guided, and that is the lamp of experience. I know of no way of judging of the future but by the past. And judging by the past, I wish to know what there has been in the conduct of the British ministry for the last ten years to justify those hopes with which gentlemen have been pleased to solace themselves and the House. Is it that insidious smile with which our petition has been lately received? Trust it not, sir; it will prove a snare to your feet. Suffer not yourselves to be betrayed with a kiss. Ask yourselves how this gracious reception of our petition comports with those warlike preparations which cover our waters and darken our land. Are fleets and armies necessary to a work of love and reconciliation? Have we shown ourselves so unwilling to be reconciled that force must be called in to win back our love?

Let us not deceive ourselves, sir. These are the implements of war and subjugation, the last arguments to which kings resort. I ask, sir, what means this martial array, if its purpose be not to force us to submission? Can gentlemen assign any other possible motive for it? Has Great Britain any enemy in this quarter of the world to call for all this accumulation of navies and armies? No, sir, she has none. They are meant for us. They can be meant for no other. They are sent over to bind and rivet upon us those chains which the British ministry have been so long forging.

And what have we to oppose to them? Shall we try argument? Sir, we have been trying that for the last ten years. Have we anything new to offer upon the subject? Nothing. We have held the subject up in every light of which it is capable; but it has been all in vain. Shall we resort to entreaty and humble supplication? What terms shall we find which have not been already exhausted? Let us not, I beseech you, sir, deceive ourselves longer. Sir, we have done everything that could be done to avert the storm which is now coming on. We have petitioned, we have remonstrated, we have supplicated, we have prostrated ourselves before the throne and have implored its interposition to arrest the tyrannical hands of the ministry and Parliament.

Name: _____ Date: _____

Speech (cont.)

Our petitions have been slighted, our remonstrances have produced additional violence and insult, our supplications have been disregarded, and we have been spurned with contempt from the foot of the throne. In vain, after these things, may we indulge the fond hope of peace and reconciliation. There is no longer any room for hope. If we wish to be free, if we mean to preserve inviolate those inestimable privileges for which we have been so long contending, if we mean not basely to abandon the noble struggle in which we have been so long engaged, and which we have pledged ourselves never to abandon until the glorious object of our contest shall be obtained, we must fight! I repeat, sir, we must fight! An appeal to arms and to the God of hosts is all that is left us.

They tell us, sir, that we are weak; unable to cope with so formidable an adversary. But when shall we be stronger? Will it be the next week or the next year? Will it be when we are totally disarmed, and when a British guard shall be stationed in every house? Shall we gather strength by irresolution and inaction? Shall we acquire the means of effectual resistance by lying supinely on our backs, and hugging the delusive phantom, hope, until our enemies shall have bound us hand and foot? Sir, we are not weak if we make a proper use of those means which the God of Nature hath placed in our power.

Three millions of people, armed in the holy cause of liberty, and in such a country as that which we possess, are invincible by any force which our enemy can send against us. Besides, sir, we shall not fight our battles alone. There is a just God who presides over the destinies of nations, and who will raise up friends to fight our battles for us. The battle, sir, is not to the strong alone; it is to the vigilant, the active, the brave. Besides, sir, we have no election. If we were base enough to desire it, it is now too late to retire from the contest. There is no retreat but in submission and slavery! Our chains are forged. Their clanking may be heard on the plains of Boston! The war is inevitable, and let it come! I repeat, sir, let it come!

It is vain, sir, to extenuate the matter. Gentlemen may cry, "Peace, Peace!" But there is no peace. The war is actually begun! The next gale that sweeps from the north will bring to our ears the clash of resounding arms! Our brethren are already in the field! Why stand we here idle? What is it that gentlemen wish? What would they have? Is life so dear, or peace so sweet, as to be purchased at the price of chains and slavery? Forbid it, Almighty God! I know not what course others may take, but as for me, give me liberty or give me death!

---

resolution – congressional bill

insidious – sinister

subjugation – suppression

entreaty – plea

remonstrated – protested

interposition – intervention

Public Domain (*Story Hour Readings* by E.C. Hartwell, 1921.)

Name: _____ Date: _____

Speech (cont.)

Assessment Questions

1. **Part A**
   Which word **best** reflects the central idea of the speech?
   - ○ A. liberty
   - ○ B. loyalty
   - ○ C. peace
   - ○ D. slavery

   Part B
   Select **two** excerpts from the speech that **best** support the answer in Part A.
   - ○ A. "Is this the part of wise men engaged in a great and arduous struggle for liberty?"
   - ○ B. "Have we shown ourselves so unwilling to be reconciled that force must be called in to win back our love?"
   - ○ C. "They are sent over to bind and rivet upon us those chains which the British ministry have been so long forging."
   - ○ D. "The war is inevitable—and let it come! I repeat, sir, let it come!"
   - ○ E. "Three millions of people, armed in the holy cause of liberty, and in such a country as that which we possess, are invincible by any force which our enemy can send against us."
   - ○ F. "The war is actually begun! The next gale that sweeps from the north will bring to our ears the clash of resounding arms!"

2. Who is the intended audience for the speech?
   - ○ A. Mr. President
   - ○ B. British Parliament
   - ○ C. King of Great Britain
   - ○ D. Virginia convention

3. **Part A**
   Which statement **best** summarizes the king's reaction to the petitions?
   - ○ A. The king graciously apologized for the grievances submitted by the Congress.
   - ○ B. The king met with Congress to discuss their grievances.
   - ○ C. The king compromised with the colonies on the issue of slavery.
   - ○ D. The king sent the British military to force the colonies into submission.

Name: _____ Date: _____

Speech (cont.)

Part B

Which excerpt from the speech **best** supports the answer in Part A?

○ A. "And judging by the past, I wish to know what there has been in the conduct of the British ministry for the last ten years to justify those hopes with which gentlemen have been pleased to solace themselves and the House."

○ B. "Is it that insidious smile with which our petition has been lately received?"

○ C. "I ask, sir, what means this martial array, if its purpose be not to force us to submission?"

○ D. "There is no retreat but in submission and slavery!"

4. Read the excerpt from the speech and answer the question.

> Let us not deceive ourselves, sir. These are the implements of war and subjugation, the last arguments to which kings resort. I ask, sir, what means this martial array, if its purpose be not to force us to <u>submission</u>? Can gentlemen assign any other possible motive for it? Has Great Britain any enemy in this quarter of the world to call for all this accumulation of navies and armies? No, sir, she has none. They are meant for us. They can be meant for no other. They are sent over to bind and rivet upon us those chains which the British ministry have been so long forging.

What is the meaning of the word <u>submission</u> as it is used in the excerpt?

○ A. to defeat an enemy

○ B. the act of yielding to someone else

○ C. to overcome an obstacle

○ D. the act of defying authority

5. Why did the speaker **most likely** use the word <u>we</u> throughout the speech?

○ A. to show that the speaker and the audience are on the same side

○ B. to demonstrate the speaker's support for the cause of liberty

○ C. to emphasize the size of the audience

○ D. to avoid addressing each member of the audience individually

Name: _____ Date: _____

Speech (cont.)

6. In his speech, Patrick Henry states, "The war is inevitable, and let it come!" Explain why Henry claims "war is inevitable." Use textual evidence from the speech to support your answer.

    Write your answer in the box.

Name: _____ Date: _____

Autobiography

Directions: Read the text and answer the questions.

Text: *Up from Slavery* by Booker T. Washington

Finally the war closed, and the day of freedom came. It was a momentous and eventful day to all upon our plantation. We had been expecting it. Freedom was in the air, and had been for months. Deserting soldiers returning to their homes were to be seen every day. Others who had been discharged, or whose regiments had been paroled, were constantly passing near our place. The "grape-vine telegraph" was kept busy night and day. The news and mutterings of great events were swiftly carried from one plantation to another. In the fear of "Yankee" invasions, the silverware and other valuables were taken from the "big house," buried in the woods, and guarded by trusted slaves. Woe be to any one who would have attempted to disturb the buried treasure. The slaves would give the Yankee soldiers food, drink, clothing—anything but that which had been specifically intrusted to their care and honour. As the great day drew nearer, there was more singing in the slave quarters than usual. It was bolder, had more ring, and lasted later into the night. Most of the verses of the plantation songs had some reference to freedom. True, they had sung those same verses before, but they had been careful to explain

that the "freedom" in these songs referred to the next world, and had no connection with life in this world. Now they gradually threw off the mask, and were not afraid to let it be known that the "freedom" in their songs meant freedom of the body in this world. The night before the eventful day, word was sent to the slave quarters to the effect that something unusual was going to take place at the "big house" the next morning. There was little, if any, sleep that night. All was excitement and expectancy. Early the next morning word was sent to

Card depicting a group of enslaved people waiting for the Emancipation Proclamation to go into effect on January 1, 1863.

all the slaves, old and young, to gather at the house. In company with my mother, brother, and sister, and a large number of other slaves, I went to the master's house. All of our master's family were either standing or seated on the veranda of the house, where they could see what was to take place and hear what was said. There was a feeling of deep interest, or perhaps sadness, on their faces, but not bitterness. As I now recall the impression they made upon me, they did not at the moment seem to be sad because of the loss of property, but rather because of parting with those whom they had reared and who were in many ways very close to them. The most distinct thing that I now recall in connection with the scene was that some man who seemed to be a stranger (a United States officer, I presume) made a little speech and then read a rather long paper—the Emancipation Proclamation, I think. After the reading we were told that we were all free, and could go when and where we pleased. My mother, who was standing

Name: _____ Date: _____

Autobiography (cont.)

by my side, leaned over and kissed her children, while tears of joy ran down her cheeks. She explained to us what it all meant, that this was the day for which she had been so long praying, but fearing that she would never live to see.

For some minutes there was great rejoicing, and thanksgiving, and wild scenes of ecstasy. But there was no feeling of bitterness. In fact, there was pity among the slaves for our former owners. The wild rejoicing on the part of the emancipated coloured people lasted but for a brief period, for I noticed that by the time they returned to their cabins there was a change in their feelings. The great responsibility of being free, of having charge of themselves, of having to think and plan for themselves and their children, seemed to take possession of them. It was very much like suddenly turning a youth of ten or twelve years out into the world to provide for himself. In a few hours the great questions with which the Anglo-Saxon race had been grappling for centuries had been thrown upon these people to be solved. These were the questions of a home, a living, the rearing of children, education, citizenship, and the establishment and support of churches. Was it any wonder that within a few hours the wild rejoicing ceased and a feeling of deep gloom seemed to pervade the slave quarters? To some it seemed that, now that they were in actual possession of it, freedom was a more serious thing than they had expected to find it. Some of the slaves were seventy or eighty years old; their best days were gone. They had no strength with which to earn a living in a strange place and among strange people, even if they had been sure where to find a new place of abode. To this class the problem seemed especially hard. Besides, deep down in their hearts there was a strange and peculiar attachment to "old Marster" and "old Missus," and to their children, which they found it hard to think of breaking off. With these they had spent in some cases nearly a half-century, and it was no light thing to think of parting. Gradually, one by one, stealthily at first, the older slaves began to wander from the slave quarters back to the "big house" to have a whispered conversation with their former owners as to the future.

Public Domain

Assessment Questions

1. Read the excerpt and answer the question.

> The "grape-vine telegraph" was kept busy night and day. The news and mutterings of great events were swiftly carried from one plantation to another.

What is the meaning of the phrase "grape-vine telegraph" as it is used in the excerpt?
- ○ A. speech given by a United States official
- ○ B. verbal information passed from one person to another
- ○ C. plantation songs of freedom
- ○ D. whispered conversations between plantation owners

Name: _____ Date: _____

Autobiography (cont.)

2. How does the author organize the details of the text?
   - ○ A. The author describes events in the order in which they occur.
   - ○ B. The author presents a problem and gives the solution.
   - ○ C. The author compares important events in his life.
   - ○ D. The author states his point of view and supports it with details.

3. **Part A**

   Which word **best** describes the theme of the text?
   - ○ A. war
   - ○ B. freedom
   - ○ C. loyalty
   - ○ D. slavery

   Part B

   Which statement from the text **best** supports the answer in Part A?
   - ○ A. "Freedom was in the air, and had been for months."
   - ○ B. "In the fear of 'Yankee' invasions, the silverware and other valuables were taken from the 'big house,' buried in the woods, and guarded by trusted slaves."
   - ○ C. "After the reading we were told that we were all free, and could go when and where we pleased."
   - ○ D. "Some of the slaves were seventy or eighty years old; their best days were gone."

4. **Part A**

   What was the purpose for the slaves gathering at the "master's house"?
   - ○ A. to hear the official announcement declaring an end to the war
   - ○ B. to celebrate the end of the war and slavery
   - ○ C. to hear the official announcement declaring an end to slavery
   - ○ D. to meet with their former owners to discuss staying on the plantation

   Part B

   Which sentence from the text **best** supports the answer in Part A?
   - ○ A. "Finally the war closed, and the day of freedom came."
   - ○ B. "After the reading we were told that we were all free, and could go when and where we pleased."
   - ○ C. "These were the questions of a home, a living, the rearing of children, education, citizenship, and the establishment and support of churches."
   - ○ D. "Gradually, one by one, stealthily at first, the older slaves began to wander from the slave quarters back to the 'big house' to have a whispered conversation with their former owners as to the future."

Name: _____ Date: _____

Autobiography (cont.)

5. What is **most likely** the author's purpose for writing the text?
   ○ A. to inform the reader about the Emancipation Proclamation
   ○ B. to emphasize to the reader the hardships of plantation life
   ○ C. to relate an important event in the author's life
   ○ D. to explain the responsibilities that come with freedom

6. Read the excerpt from the text and answer the question.

> Gradually, one by one, stealthily at first, the older slaves began to wander from the slave quarters back to the "big house" to have a whispered conversation with their former owners as to the future.

What can the reader **most likely** infer from the excerpt?
   ○ A. Older slaves were eager to start their new lives away from the plantation.
   ○ B. Older slaves were afraid to let the younger slaves see them go to the "big house."
   ○ C. Older slaves were concerned about their new lives as free men and women.
   ○ D. Older slaves were eager to celebrate with their former owners.

7. Based on the text, explain why the mood of the slaves changed from "wild rejoicing" to "a feeling of deep gloom." Support your answer with details from the text.

Write your answer in the box.

Name: _____ Date: _____

Science Article

Directions: Read the text and answer the questions.

Text: "Pacific Salmon" (excerpt) (U.S. Fish & Wildlife Service National Digital Library)

The upriver salmon migration is one of nature's most exciting dramas. But to the seven species of Pacific salmon (chinook, chum, coho, pink and sockeye salmon, as well as sea-run cutthroat and steelhead trout), it is a long, strenuous and desperate race against time, with every obstacle taking its toll.

Pacific salmon belong to a group called *anadromous* fish that includes Atlantic salmon, sturgeon, lampreys, shad and herring. Anadromous fish hatch and live the first part of their lives in fresh water, then migrate to the ocean to spend their adult lives, which may be as short as 6 months or as long as 7 years. When they reach sexual maturity, they return to the freshwater stream of their origin to lay their eggs. Although Atlantic salmon may repeat this cycle several times, Pacific salmon make the round trip only once.

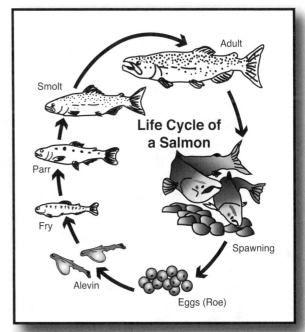

Migration between fresh and salt water occurs during every season of the year, depending on the latitude and genetic characteristics of the fish. Groups of fish that migrate together are called *runs* or *stocks*. Salmon spawn in virtually all types of freshwater habitat, from intertidal areas to high mountain streams. Pacific salmon may swim thousands of miles to get back to the stream where they hatched.

However, only a small percentage of salmon live to reach their natal stream or spawning ground. Those males that survive the trip are often gaunt, with grotesquely humped backs, hooked jaws and battle-torn fins. The females are swollen with a pound or more of eggs. Both have large white patches of bruised skin on their backs and sides.

Since salmon do not feed after they leave the ocean, some die on the way to spawn because they lack enough stored body fat to make the trip. Many become caught in fishermen's nets. Those that evade the nets may have to swim through polluted waters near cities. Many make their way over power dams, leaping up from one tiny pool to the next along cement stairstep cascades called *fish ladders*. In the tributary streams, waterfalls and rapids are steep and swift enough to eliminate all but the strongest salmon. Otters, eagles and bears stalk the salmon in shallow riffles. Once on the spawning grounds, the fish battle each other: females against females for places to nest, males against males for available females.

The female builds her nest, called a *redd*, by agitating the bottom gravel with her fins and tail and bending her body into a U shape first one way, then the other. As soon as she has excavated a depression, she settles into it and deposits her first batch of eggs, or *roe*. The male then moves alongside and deposits *milt* over the roe. The female rakes her tail back and forth to cover the redd with loose gravel. She then excavates her next redd a short distance upstream.

Name: _____ Date: _____

Science Article (cont.)

The process continues until all the roe and milt have been deposited. One pair of salmon may have as many as seven redds, though four or five is average. The salmon die within a few days of spawning.

The translucent salmon eggs range in color from pale yellowish-orange to dark reddish-orange. The color varies both by species and within species and is determined by water temperature, sediment composition, age and other factors. The eggs vary in size from the tiny sockeye roe (about 1/4 inch) to the large chum roe (almost 1/2 inch).

Incubation time ranges from 5 to 10 weeks. The newly hatched fish are called *fry* or *sac fry* because they continue to feed on the yolk sac attached to their bellies. Depending on water temperature, species and other factors, they may stay in the gravel for several weeks before swimming up into the open water of the stream, where they feed on plankton and other tiny aquatic organisms. By the time they reach fingerling size (about 3 inches), most pink and chum salmon have begun the long journey downstream and out to sea. Sockeye, coho and most chinook spend from 1 to 2 years in fresh water before heading out to sea.

As the stream current carries the young salmon to the ocean, where they will spend the majority of their lives, their bodies undergo *smoltation*, physical and chemical changes that enable them to survive in salt water.

Most adult Pacific salmon species feed on aquatic insects and small fish. However, sockeye are filter feeders. They take in water full of plankton, and as the water flows back out of their mouths, specialized organs called *gill rakers* act like strainers, holding the plankton in to be swallowed.

Some species of Pacific salmon stay within a few hundred miles of their home river, while others disperse north, south, west, or in the case of salmon originating in Russian and Japanese rivers and streams, east into feeding grounds in the Aleutian islands and other areas of the north Pacific. Chinook salmon may travel as far as 2,500 miles from their home stream and stay out at sea 4 to 7 years. Pink salmon, on the other hand, seldom range more than 150 miles from the mouth of their home river or stream where they hatch in the fall, and turn homeward in the spring, sometimes traveling 45 miles per day to reach their spawning grounds.

Pacific salmon encounter increasing human-caused hazards in their migrations to and from spawning grounds. All salmonids require pure, well-oxygenated cold water and are one of the first species to suffer when water quality is degraded. Many salmon stocks are seriously threatened by habitat destruction, hydroelectric dams on migratory rivers, harvest of rare stocks and competition with hatchery fish. Some stocks are so severely reduced that they have been listed as endangered or threatened species under the Endangered Species Act. *Endangered* means they are likely to become extinct. *Threatened* means they are likely to become endangered in the near future.

Public Domain

Name: _____ Date: _____

Science Article (cont.)

Assessment Questions

1. Based on the text, what is the difference between the Pacific salmon and the Atlantic salmon?
   - ○ A. The Pacific salmon stay within a few hundred miles of their home river, while the Atlantic salmon travel east into feeding grounds in the Aleutian islands.
   - ○ B. The Pacific salmon population is seriously threatened by habitat destruction, while the Atlantic salmon population is threatened by construction of hydroelectric dams on migratory rivers.
   - ○ C. The Pacific salmon return to the freshwater stream of their origins to lay their eggs only once, while the Atlantic salmon make the trip several times.
   - ○ D. The Pacific salmon feed on aquatic insects, while the Atlantic salmon feed on plankton.

2. Which word **best** describes the tone of the passage?
   - ○ A. informative
   - ○ B. nostalgic
   - ○ C. pleasant
   - ○ D. sincere

3. Read the sentence from the text and answer the question.

> Many salmon stocks are seriously threatened by <u>habitat</u> destruction, hydroelectric dams on migratory rivers, harvest of rare stocks and competition with hatchery fish.

   Which word is a synonym for <u>habitat</u> as it is used in the sentence?
   - ○ A. area
   - ○ B. environment
   - ○ C. location
   - ○ D. water

4. What is the author's purpose for writing the article?
   - ○ A. to persuade the reader to support Pacific salmon conservation programs
   - ○ B. to describe to the reader the life cycle and migration of Pacific salmon
   - ○ C. to inform the reader about the impact man has had on the Pacific salmon population
   - ○ D. to inform the reader about hazards Pacific salmon encounter during migration

Name: _____ Date: _____

Science Article (cont.)

5. Why did the author **most likely** include the "Life Cycle of the Pacific Salmon" diagram in the article?
    - ○ A. to illustrate the size of salmon at each stage of life
    - ○ B. to emphasize the importance of the salmon's adult stage of life
    - ○ C. to illustrate the stages in the life of the Pacific salmon
    - ○ D. to provide a visual image of Pacific salmon fry

6. What is the incubation time for salmon *roe*?
    - ○ A. 5–10 weeks
    - ○ B. 6 months
    - ○ C. 1 year
    - ○ D. 2 years

7. How does the author organize the information in the excerpt?
    - ○ A. The author lists the hazards faced by migrating salmon.
    - ○ B. The author argues the need for Pacific salmon conservation programs and supports it with evidence.
    - ○ C. The author uses details to describe the upriver migration of the Pacific salmon.
    - ○ D. The author uses details to describe the life cycle and migration of Pacific salmon.

8. Based on the text, what factors have contributed to the near-extinction of the Pacific salmon population? Use information from the text to support your answer.

    Write your answer in the box.

Name: _____ Date: _____

Newspaper Article

Directions: Read the text and answer the questions.

Text: "The Rights of Women" by Fredrick Douglass

(The following editorial was written by Frederick Douglass and published in his newspaper, *The North Star*, on July 28, 1848.)

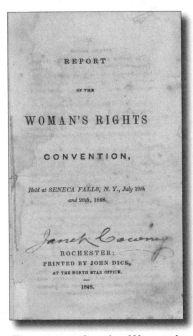

The report for the Woman's Rights Convention was printed at The North Star offices.

THE RIGHTS OF WOMEN.—One of the most interesting events of the past week, was the holding of what is technically styled a Woman's Rights Convention at Seneca Falls. The speaking, addresses, and resolutions of this extraordinary meeting were almost wholly conducted by women; and although they evidently felt themselves in a novel position, it is but simple justice to say that their whole proceedings were characterized by marked ability and dignity. No one present, we think, however much he might be disposed to differ from the views advanced by the leading speakers on that occasion, will fail to give them credit for brilliant talents and excellent dispositions. In this meeting, as in other deliberative assemblies, there were frequent differences of opinion and animated discussion; but in no case was there the slightest absence of good feeling and decorum. Several interesting documents setting forth the rights as well as grievances of women were read. Among these was a Declaration of Sentiments, to be regarded as the basis of a grand movement for attaining the civil, social, political, and religious rights of women. We should not do justice to our own convictions, or to the excellent persons connected with this infant movement, if we did not in this connection offer a few remarks on the general subject which the Convention met to consider and the objects they seek to attain. A discussion of the rights of animals would be regarded with far more complacency by many of what are called the *wise* and the *good* of our land, than would be a discussion of the rights of women. It is, in their estimation, to be guilty of evil thoughts, to think that woman is entitled to equal rights with man. Many who have at last made the discovery that the negroes have some rights as well as other members of the human family, have yet to be convinced that women are entitled to any. Eight years ago a number of persons of this description actually abandoned the anti-slavery cause, lest by giving their influence in that direction they might possibly be giving countenance to the dangerous heresy that woman, in respect to rights, stands on an equal footing with man. In the judgment of such persons the American slave system, with all its concomitant horrors, is less to be deplored than this wicked idea. It is perhaps needless to say, that we cherish little sympathy for such sentiments or respect for such prejudices. Standing as we do upon the watch-tower of human freedom, we can not be deterred from an expression of our approbation of any movement, however humble, to improve and elevate the character of any members of the human family. While it is impossible for us to go into this subject at length, and dispose of the various objections which are often urged against such a doctrine as that of female equality, we are free to say that in respect to

Name: _____ Date: _____

Newspaper Article (cont.)

political rights, we hold woman to be justly entitled to all we claim for man. We go farther, and express our conviction that all political rights which it is expedient for man to exercise, it is equally so for woman. All that distinguishes man as an intelligent and accountable being, is equally true of woman; and if that government only is just which governs by the free consent of the governed, there can be no reason in the world for denying to woman the exercise of the elective franchise, or a hand in making and administering the laws of the land. Our doctrine is that "right is of no sex." We therefore bid the women engaged in this movement our humble Godspeed.

Frederick Douglass

complacency – self-satisfaction

concomitant – associated

approbation – approval

Public Domain (*History of Women's Suffrage: Volume 1,* edited by Elizabeth Cady Stanton, 1889)

Assessment Questions

1. **Part A**
   Which phrase **best** describes the central idea of the newspaper editorial?
   - ○ A. support for the women's rights movement
   - ○ B. writing of the Declaration of Sentiments
   - ○ C. injustice of the American slave trade
   - ○ D. holding of the Woman's Rights Convention

   Part B
   Which sentence from the text **best** supports the answer in Part A?
   - ○ A. "One of the most interesting events of the past week, was the holding of what is technically styled a Woman's Rights Convention at Seneca Falls."
   - ○ B. "Among these was a Declaration of Sentiments, to be regarded as the basis of a grand movement for attaining the civil, social, political, and religious rights of women."
   - ○ C. "In the judgment of such persons the American slave system, with all its concomitant horrors, is less to be deplored than this wicked idea."
   - ○ D. "Standing as we do upon the watch-tower of human freedom, we can not be deterred from an expression of our approbation of any movement, however humble, to improve and elevate the character of any members of the human family."

2. What is the author's **main** purpose for writing the text?
   - ○ A. to persuade readers to support the women's rights movement
   - ○ B. to express to readers his support for the women's rights movement
   - ○ C. to express his feelings about the political rights of women
   - ○ D. to describe the events of the first Woman's Rights Convention

Name: _____ Date: _____

Newspaper Article (cont.)

3. Read the excerpt from the text and answer the question.

> In this meeting, as in other <u>deliberative</u> assemblies, there were frequent differences of opinion and animated discussion; but in no case was there the slightest absence of good feeling and decorum.

Part A
What is the **best** meaning for the word <u>deliberative</u> as it is used in the excerpt?
- ○ A. stating an opinion
- ○ B. stating an argument
- ○ C. engaging in public speaking
- ○ D. engaging in debate and dialogue

Part B
Which **two** phrases from the excerpt **best** support the answer in Part A?

Write the answer in the box.

```



```

4. **Part A**
Which word **best** describes the tone of the text?
- ○ A. admiring
- ○ B. caring
- ○ C. impartial
- ○ D. supportive

Part B
Which sentence from the text **best** supports the answer in Part A?
- ○ A. "…it is but simple justice to say that their whole proceedings were characterized by marked ability and dignity."
- ○ B. "Several interesting documents setting forth the rights as well as grievances of women were read."
- ○ C. "It is, in their estimation, to be guilty of evil thoughts, to think that woman is entitled to equal rights with man."
- ○ D. "We go farther, and express our conviction that all political rights which it is expedient for man to exercise, it is equally so for woman."

Name: _____ Date: _____

Newspaper Article (cont.)

5. Read the excerpt and answer the question.

> A discussion of the rights of animals would be regarded with far more complacency by many of what are called the *wise* and the *good* of our land, than would be a discussion of the rights of women. It is, in their estimation, to be guilty of evil thoughts, to think that woman is entitled to equal rights with man.

What can the reader **most likely** conclude about public opinion concerning women's rights?

○ A. Only women supported equal rights for women.
○ B. A majority of the public supported equal rights for women.
○ C. People were divided on the issue of women's rights.
○ D. Most people had no opinion on the issue of women's rights.

6. Based on the editorial, what effect did the women's rights movement have on the anti-slavery cause? Use information from the text to support your answer.

Write your answer in the box.

Name: _____ Date: _____

Flyer

10th Annual Statewide Middle School Science Fair
University Plaza Auditorium
Saturday, June 17, 8:00 A.M. – 3:00 P.M.

The statewide science fair is an opportunity for students to apply the scientific method to conduct independent research. The purpose of the fair is to motivate students to explore the world around them.

Setup Time
All project displays must be set up in the University Plaza Auditorium between the hours of 3:30 P.M. and 7:30 P.M. on Friday, June 16.

Project Categories
Biology   Chemistry
Energy   Engineering
Physics   Environmental Science
Earth and Space Science

Eligibility Requirements (No exceptions will be granted.)
A student may choose to enter one individual project or be a member of a team. A team project will consist of two or three students. All projects must follow the scientific method.

Basic Exhibit Rules
For safety reasons, certain items are not allowed to be used or displayed at the science fair. Drawings, photos, diagrams, or models should be used instead.

Items Not Allowed
- any type of cultured growth, spoiled food, or molds
- living creatures (animals or microorganisms)
- human or animal tissues such as teeth, hair, nails, or animal bones
- taxidermy items, preserved animals, or embryos
- chemicals of any kind
- food (human or animal)
- sharp instruments such as syringes, needles, or pipettes
- poisons, drugs, controlled substances

Prizes
Grand Prize: Trip to Washington D.C.

1st Place: $1,000 Savings Bond
2nd Place: $250 Savings Bond
3rd Place: $100 Savings Bond

Trophies and ribbons will be awarded for each project category.

Entry Forms
- Starting April 14, entry forms are available online at: <http://ssf.gov/application.pdf>.
- Email entry forms no later than May 1 to: <sbarnes@ssf.gov>.
- For more information: Contact Sue Barnes at 417-SCIENCE or visit the website at: <http://ssf.gov/>.

*All projects will be judged for scientific merit using the same criteria regardless of the number of individuals preparing the project.

Name: _____ Date: _____

Flyer (cont.)

Assessment Questions

1. Read the sentence from the flyer and answer the question.

> All projects will be judged for scientific <u>merit</u> using the same criteria regardless of the number of individuals preparing the project.

    What is the **best** meaning of the word <u>merit</u> as it is used in the excerpt?
    ○ A. appeal
    ○ B. importance
    ○ C. interest
    ○ D. worth

2. According to the flyer, what should a student do if they need additional information about the statewide science fair?
    ○ A. ask their science teacher
    ○ B. contact the University Plaza
    ○ C. email <sbarnes@ssf.gov>
    ○ D. visit the website at: <http://ssf.gov/>

3. Based on the exhibit rules, which item is not allowed to be displayed at the science fair?
    ○ A. live animals
    ○ B. beakers
    ○ C. plants
    ○ D. water samples

4. What is the earliest date science fair entry forms will be available online?
    ○ A. April 14
    ○ B. May 1
    ○ C. June 16
    ○ D. June 17

5. What is the author's purpose for creating the flyer?
    ○ A. to persuade the reader to attend the statewide science fair
    ○ B. to provide information to the reader about the statewide science fair
    ○ C. to inform the reader about the type of items that can be displayed
    ○ D. to encourage the reader to investigate the field of environmental science

6. Which word **best** describes the tone of the flyer?
    ○ A. formal
    ○ B. friendly
    ○ C. informative
    ○ D. persuasive

Name: _____ Date: _____

Flyer (cont.)

7. **Part A**

Based on the flyer, what can the reader **most likely** conclude about a team project with four members?

- ○ A. The team will need to contact Sue Barnes for special permission to enter.
- ○ B. The team's project will be judged using different criteria.
- ○ C. The team's project display will take too long to set up.
- ○ D. The team will not be allowed to enter a project in the science fair.

Part B

Which **two** statements from the text **best** support the answer in Part A?

- ○ A. "All project displays must be set up in the University Plaza Auditorium between the hours of 3:30 P.M. to 7:30 P.M. on Friday, June 16."
- ○ B. "No exceptions will be granted."
- ○ C. "A student may choose to enter one individual project or be a member of a team."
- ○ D. "A team project will consist of two or three students."
- ○ E. "For more information: Contact Sue Barnes at 417-SCIENCE…"
- ○ F. "All projects will be judged for scientific merit using the same criteria…"

8. What would **most likely** be a student's incentive for entering the statewide science fair? Use information from the flyer to support your answer.

Write your answer in the box.

Name: _____ Date: _____

Paired Text

Directions: Read **Text One** and answer the questions.

Text One: "Great Commander of the Union Armies" by William H. Mace
(Secondary Source)

President Lincoln saw that General Ulysses Grant was a great soldier. He sent for him to come to Washington and made him lieutenant-general in command of all the armies of the United States.

General Grant was elected President in 1868, three years after the end of the Civil War.

Grant took command at once. His first great object was to capture Lee's army. The shortest way to Lee's army lay through the "Wilderness," a part of the country lying south of the upper part of the Rapidan, in Virginia, and covered with a thick forest of tangled underbrush. The route was dangerous. But into the "Wilderness" Grant plunged with his great army. General Lee was there with his troops. The fighting began. For a month it was almost constant charging, back and forth, and there were long lists of dead and wounded. Grant moved his army southward and nearer Richmond. Lee met him in the bloody battles of Spottsylvania and Cold Harbor.

Then Grant crossed the James River, south of Richmond, and began the attack on Petersburg. This place was taken in the spring of 1865.

General Lee told the Confederate president, Jefferson Davis, that he could hold Richmond no longer. He tried to get his army away, but the men were weak from hard fighting, and Sheridan, with his cavalry, was too quick for him.

General Grant wrote to General Lee suggesting that he surrender, and thus prevent the loss of more lives. Lee agreed, and the papers were signed April 9, 1865, at Appomattox Court House. No more generous terms were ever given than those granted to Lee and his men.

After the war was over General Grant served for a time in the cabinet of President Johnson, who had become president at Lincoln's death. In 1868, he was elected President of the United States.

---

cavalry – branch of the army that fought mainly on horseback

Public Domain ("Two Great Generals." *A Beginner's History* by William H. Mace, 1916).

Name: _____ Date: _____

Paired Text (cont.)

Assessment Questions

Use Text One, "Great Commander of the Union Armies," to answer questions 1–5.

1. According to the text, what was General Grant's **primary** objective after taking command of the Union armies?
   - ○ A. to meet with President Lincoln
   - ○ B. to ask General Lee to surrender
   - ○ C. to capture General Lee's army
   - ○ D. to prevent the loss of soldiers' lives

2. What is the author's purpose for writing the text?
   - ○ A. to persuade the reader that Grant was a better general than Lee
   - ○ B. to explain to the reader the terms of the surrender agreement
   - ○ C. to inform the reader about the events leading up to the surrender of General Lee
   - ○ D. to compare the leadership styles of Grant and Lee

3. Which word **best** describes the tone of the text?
   - ○ A. informative
   - ○ B. judgmental
   - ○ C. sentimental
   - ○ D. sincere

4. Which statement from the text is an opinion?
   - ○ A. "Lee met him in the bloody battles of Spottsylvania and Cold Harbor."
   - ○ B. "Lee agreed, and the papers were signed April 9, 1865, at Appomattox Court House."
   - ○ C. "No more generous terms were ever given than those granted to Lee and his men."
   - ○ D. "In 1868, he was elected President of the United States."

5. According to the text, what are **two** reasons that General Lee **most likely** surrendered to General Grant?
   - ○ A. General Lee's men were worn out from hard fighting, so he was unable to retreat.
   - ○ B. General Lee wanted to prevent further loss of life.
   - ○ C. Sheridan's cavalry prevented General Lee's efforts to retreat.
   - ○ D. Jefferson Davis, the Confederate President, ordered General Lee to surrender.
   - ○ E. General Lee knew General Grant would be generous with the terms of surrender.
   - ○ F. General Lee was tired of fighting and wanted to return home.

Name: _____ Date: _____

Paired Text (cont.)

Directions: Read **Text Two** and answer the questions.

Text Two: *Personal Memoirs of U. S. Grant* by Ulysses S. Grant
(Primary Source)

...I found him [Lee] at the house of a Mr. McLean, at Appomattox Court House, with Colonel Marshall, one of his staff officers, awaiting my arrival... We greeted each other, and after shaking hands took our seats. I had my staff with me, a good portion of whom were in the room during the whole of the interview.

We soon fell into a conversation about old army times...Our conversation grew so pleasant that I almost forgot the object of our meeting. After the conversation had run on in this style for some time, General Lee called my attention to the object of our meeting, and said that he had asked for this interview for the purpose of getting from me the terms I proposed to give his army. I said that I meant merely that his army should lay down their arms, not to take them up again during the continuance of the war unless duly and properly exchanged. He said that he had so understood my letter. Then we gradually fell off again into conversation about matters foreign to the subject which had brought us together...General Lee again interrupted the course of the conversation by suggesting that the terms I proposed to give his army ought to be written out. I called to General Parker, secretary on my staff, for writing materials, and commenced writing out the following terms:

APPOMATTOX C. H., VA.,
Ap 9th, 1865.

GEN. R. E. LEE,
Comd'g C. S. A.
    GEN: In accordance with the substance of my letter to you of the 8th inst. [instant], I propose to receive the surrender of the Army of N. Va. on the following terms, to wit: Rolls of all the officers and men to be made in duplicate. One copy to be given to an officer designated by me, the other to be retained by such officer or officers as you may designate. The officers to give their individual paroles not to take up arms against the Government of the United States until properly exchanged, and each company or regimental commander sign a like parole for the men of their commands. The arms, artillery and public property to be parked and stacked, and turned over to the officer appointed by me to receive them. This will not embrace the side-arms of the officers, nor their private horses or baggage. This done, each officer and man will be allowed to return to their homes, not to be disturbed by United States authority so long as they observe their paroles and the laws in force where they may reside.

Very respectfully,

U. S. GRANT,
Lt. Gen.

Paired Text (cont.)

When I put my pen to the paper I did not know the first word that I should make use of in writing the terms. I only knew what was in my mind, and I wished to express it clearly, so that there could be no mistaking it. As I wrote on, the thought occurred to me that the officers had their own private horses and effects, which were important to them, but of no value to us; also that it would be an unnecessary humiliation to call upon them to deliver their side arms.

The surrender of Lee's Army of Northern Virginia at Appomattox Court House, Virginia, on April 9, 1865. Seated left to right: General Ulysses S. Grant, General Robert E. Lee

No conversation, not one word, passed between General Lee and myself, either about private property, side arms, or kindred subjects. He appeared to have no objections to the terms first proposed; or if he had a point to make against them he wished to wait until they were in writing to make it. When he read over that part of the terms about side arms, horses and private property of the officers, he remarked, with some feeling, I thought, that this would have a happy effect upon his army.

Then, after a little further conversation, General Lee remarked to me again that their army was organized a little differently from the army of the United States (still maintaining by implication that we were two countries); that in their army the cavalrymen and artillerists owned their own horses; and he asked if he was to understand that the men who so owned their horses were to be permitted to retain them. I told him that as the terms were written they would not; that only the officers were permitted to take their private property. He then, after reading over the terms a second time, remarked that that was clear.

I then said to him that I thought this would be about the last battle of the war—I sincerely hoped so; and I said further I took it that most of the men in the ranks were small farmers. The whole country had been so raided by the two armies that it was doubtful whether they would be able to put in a crop to carry themselves and their families through the next winter without the aid of the horses they were then riding. The United States did not want them and I would, therefore, instruct the officers I left behind to receive the paroles of his troops to let every man of the Confederate army who claimed to own a horse or mule take the animal to his home. Lee remarked again that this would have a happy effect.

Public Domain

Name: _____ Date: _____

Paired Text (cont.)

Assessment Questions

Use Text Two, **Personal Memoirs of U. S. Grant,** *to answer questions 6–9.*

6. Which word **best** describes the tone of the text?
   - ○ A. arrogant
   - ○ B. condescending
   - ○ C. sincere
   - ○ D. sympathetic

7. **Part A**
   According to the text, who proposed the terms of surrender?
   - ○ A. General Grant
   - ○ B. President Lincoln
   - ○ C. General Lee
   - ○ D. General Parker

   Part B
   Which sentence from the text **best** supports the answer in Part A?
   - ○ A. "I had my staff with me, a good portion of whom were in the room during the whole of the interview."
   - ○ B. "When I put my pen to the paper I did not know the first word that I should make use of in writing the terms."
   - ○ C. "General Lee called my attention to the object of our meeting, and said that he had asked for this interview for the purpose of getting from me the terms I proposed to give his army."
   - ○ D. "No conversation, not one word, passed between General Lee and myself, either about private property, side arms, or kindred subjects."

8. Read the excerpt and answer the question.

> Then, after a little further conversation, General Lee remarked to me again that their army was organized a little differently from the army of the United States (still maintaining by implication that we were two countries); . . .

   What does this excerpt reveal about General Lee?
   - ○ A. General Lee did not consider himself to be a citizen of the United States.
   - ○ B. General Lee felt Confederate troops were better organized than Union troops.
   - ○ C. General Lee believed the United States Army was inferior to the Confederate Army.
   - ○ D. General Lee regretted his role in the Civil War.

Name: _____ Date: _____

Paired Text (cont.)

9. Which sentence reveals the structure used to organize the text?
   - ○ A. General Grant describes the terms of paroles for Confederate soldiers.
   - ○ B. General Grant proposes a solution to end the Civil War.
   - ○ C. General Grant describes the effects of war on Confederate soldiers.
   - ○ D. General Grant relates the order of events in his interview with General Lee.

Assessment Questions

Use Text One and Text Two to answer question 10.

10. In **Text One** (secondary source), the author states, "No more generous terms were ever given than those granted to Lee and his men." What evidence from **Text Two** (primary source) supports this claim?

    Write your answer in the box.

Answer Keys

Instructional Resources

<u>Reading Comprehension</u> (p. 6)
  Answer: D
<u>Making Inferences</u> (p. 7)
  Answer: Part A: B; Part B: A
<u>Textual Evidence</u> (p. 8)
  Answer: "Five hundred millions in property was destroyed," and "two hundred and fifty thousand
      people were left homeless and without food."
<u>Theme</u> (p. 9)
  Answer: Part A: C; Part B: (Answers will vary.)
<u>Central Idea</u> (p. 10)
  Answer: C
<u>Summary</u> (p. 11)
  Answer: A, F
<u>Word Meaning</u> (p. 12)
  Answer: Part A: C; Part B: C, D
<u>Tone</u> (p. 13)
  Answer: Part A: B; Part B: D, E
<u>Author's Purpose</u> (p. 14)
  Answer: C
<u>Point of View</u> (p. 15)
  Answer: A
<u>Organizational Text Structures</u> (p. 16)
  Answer: A
<u>Structure of Poetry</u> (p. 17)
  Answer: 1. four   2. four   3. Answers will vary.   4. bright

Practice Assessments
Literature

<u>Novel</u> (p. 20–23)
  1.   D 2. C 3. A 4. B 5. D 6. A 7. B 8. D; B 9. B
  10. (Answers will vary but should include) If you read Excerpt 2 only, the reader might assume
       that Buck seized Thornton's hand in his teeth out of excitement. After reading Excerpt 1,
       you understand that Buck's seizing of "Thornton's hand in his teeth" in Excerpt 2 was his
       method of expressing his love for John Thornton, since he wasn't able to express it with
       speech.

<u>Poem</u> (p. 24–26)
  1.   B, D 2. A 3. C; D 4. D 5. A 6. D; C
  7.   (Answers will vary but should include) In stanza 4, the speaker says that often when he is at
       home, lying on his couch in a "pensive mood," the memory of the daffodils will "flash upon
       his inward eye." He describes this as the "bliss of solitude." The joy of the memory gives
       him pleasure and his heart "dances with the daffodils." In stanza 3, the speaker states that
       while he "gazed—and gazed" on the daffodils, he didn't think anything about the "wealth
       the show to me had brought." The reader now understands that the insignificant event did
       become an important event, because the "wealth" mentioned in stanza 3 is the joy the
       speaker receives from recalling the memory of the daffodils.

Drama (p. 31–33)
1. C   2. D   3. A   4. B   5. A   6. D
7. (Answers will vary but should include) The White Queen knows what is going to happen and reacts to events because she has already lived through them. The White Queen's shawl comes flying in, and Alice catches it. Alice helps the White Queen put on her shawl. As she is talking to Alice, the White Queen begins wrapping a cloth around her finger and "binds the cloth with a ribbon." The White Queen then lets out a shrill scream, and cries out "my finger's bleeding." Alice then asks the White Queen if she has pricked her finger. The White Queen replies, "I haven't pricked it YET—but I soon shall." Then her brooch flies open and the White Queen "clutches it wildly." She pricks her finger and it starts bleeding. The White Queen turns to Alice and says, "That accounts for the bleeding, you see. Now you understand the way things happen here." Alice asks her why isn't she screaming. The White Queen replies, "Why, I've done all the screaming already."

Informational Text

Speech (p. 36–38)
1. A; A, E   2. D   3. D; C   4. B   5. A
6. (Answers will vary but may include) Patrick Henry claims "war is inevitable." He states that the petitions of the colonies have been met with the "warlike preparations" that cover the "waters and darken our land". He asks, "what means this martial array, if its purpose be not to force us to submission?" He states, "Our petitions have been slighted, our remonstrances have produced additional violence and insult, our supplications have been disregarded, and we have been spurned with contempt from the foot of the throne." Henry states, "There is no longer any room for hope." He argues, "'Peace, Peace!' But there is no peace. The war is actually begun!"

Autobiography (p. 40–42)
1. B   2. A   3. B; A   4. C; B   5. C   6. C
7. (Answers will vary but may include) After the reading of the Emancipation Proclamation there was "great rejoicing, and thanksgiving, and wild scenes of ecstasy." Toward their former owners, the freed slaves felt no "bitterness" only "pity." The mood changes when a "feeling of deep gloom" set in once the freed slaves realized the "great responsibility" that came with "having to think and plan for themselves and their children." This type of responsibility was something they had never been taught or allowed to do for themselves. The responsibility of "freedom was a more serious thing than they had expected."

Science Article (p. 45–46)
1. C   2. A   3. B   4. B   5. C   6. A   7. D
8. (Answers will vary but may include) There are several factors that have contributed to the near-extinction of the Pacific salmon population. The salmon face many hazards caused by humans in their migration to and from their spawning grounds: poor "water quality," "habitat destruction, hydroelectric dams on migratory rivers, harvest of rare stocks and competition with hatchery fish."

Newspaper Article (p. 48–50)
1. A; D   2. B   3. D; "differences of opinion" and "animated discussion"
4. D; D   5. C
6. (Answers will vary but may include) According to Frederick Douglass, the women's rights movement had a negative effect on the anti-slavery cause. Many who supported the anti-slavery cause abandoned the movement when the issue of women's rights emerged. These supporters felt that people would think they also supported women's rights.

Flyer (Functional Text) (p. 52–53)
1. D   2. D   3. A   4. A   5. B   6. C   7. D; B, D
8. (Answers will vary but may include) The prizes would most likely motivate a student to enter the science fair. The Grand Prize is a trip to "Washington D.C." The first-place winner will receive a "$1,000 Savings Bond," second-place winner will receive a "$250 Savings Bond," and third-place winner will receive a "$100 Savings Bond."

Paired Text
Text One (p. 55)
1. C   2. C   3. A   4. C   5. A, C
Text Two (p. 58–59)
6. C   7. A; C   8. A   9. D
Text One and Text Two (p. 59)
10. (Answers will vary but may include) There are three examples that support the claim that General Grant was very generous with his terms of surrender. First, he allowed the officers to keep their horses, private property, and side arms. General Grant felt that it would humiliate the officers by asking them for their side arms. Second, while he could have imprisoned the Confederate troops, he decided to parole any soldier who agreed to "lay down their arms, not to take them up again during the continuance of the war unless duly and properly exchanged." They would be allowed to return home and wouldn't "be disturbed by United States authority" as long as they observed the conditions of their parole. The third example of his generosity was when General Lee asked if all the men got to keep their horses. At first, General Grant said only the officers would be allowed to keep their horses. He then reconsidered and said he would "let every man of the Confederate army who claimed to own a horse or mule take the animal to his home." He knew most of these men were small farmers and would need the animals to work the fields when they returned home.